RECORDED VERSIONS
GUITAR

AUTHENTIC TRANSCRIPTIONS
WITH NOTES AND TABLATURE

**Transcribed By
PETE BILLMANN
and
STEVE GORENBERG**

NIRVANA UNPLUGGED IN NEW YORK

**Photos by Jennifer Youngblood-Grohl
Cover Photo by Frank Micelotta**

ISBN 0-7935-4413-0

HAL•LEONARD™
CORPORATION
7777 W. BLUEMOUND RD. P.O. BOX 13819 MILWAUKEE, WI 53213

RECORDED VERSIONS GUITAR

AUTHENTIC TRANSCRIPTIONS
WITH NOTES AND TABLATURE

NIRVANA UNPLUGGED IN NEW YORK

CONTENTS

About A Girl

By Kurt Cobain

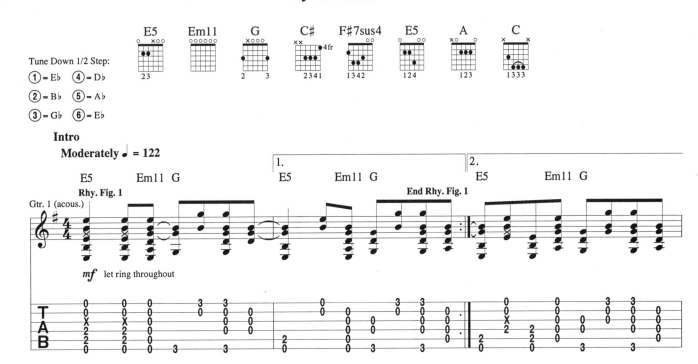

Tune Down 1/2 Step:
① = Eb ④ = Db
② = Bb ⑤ = Ab
③ = Gb ⑥ = Eb

Intro

Moderately ♩ = 122

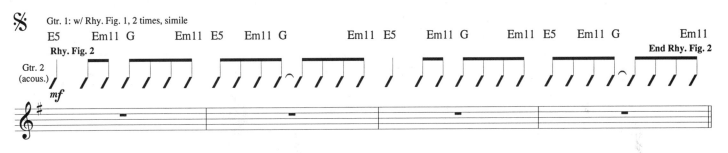

Verse

Gtr. 1: w/ Rhy. Fig. 1, 4 times, simile
Gtr. 2: w/ Rhy. Fig. 2, 2 times, simile

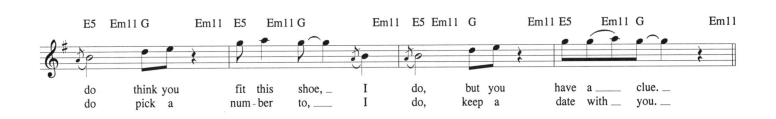

1.,3. I need an eas-y friend, I do, with an ear to ___ lend. ___ I
2. I'm stand-ing in your line. I do hope you have the ___ time. ___ I

do think you fit this shoe, ___ I do, but you have a ___ clue. ___
do pick a num-ber to, ___ I do, keep a date with ___ you. ___

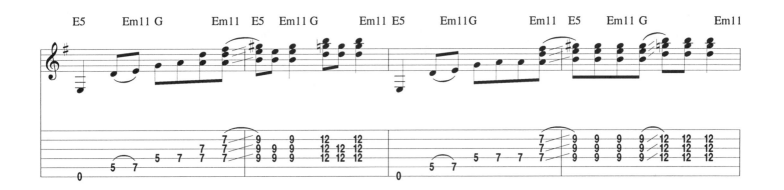

Gtrs. 1 & 2: w/ Rhy. Figs. 3 & 3A, simile

D.S. al Coda

Coda

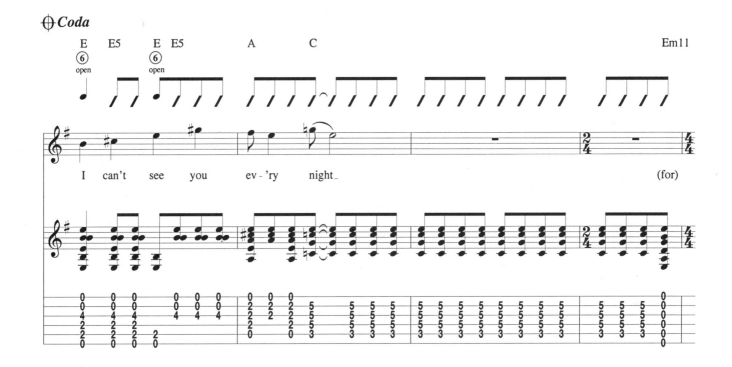

I can't see you ev-'ry night (for)

Gtr. 1: w/ Rhy. Fig. 1, 4 times, simile
Gtr. 2: w/ Rhy. Fig. 2, 2 times, simile

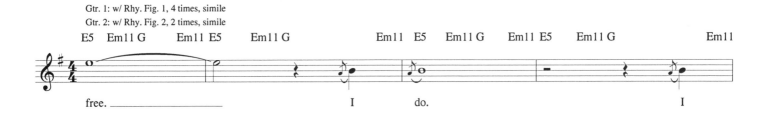

free. _____ I do. I

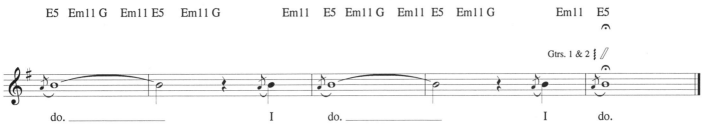

do. _____ I do. _____ I do.

Come As You Are

By Kurt Cobain

Bridge

And I swear that __ I don't __ have a gun. __ No, I don't __

To Coda ⊕

(Gtr. 1 cont. in notation)

__ have a gun. __ No, I don't __ have a gun. __

Gtr. 2: w/ Riff 1A,

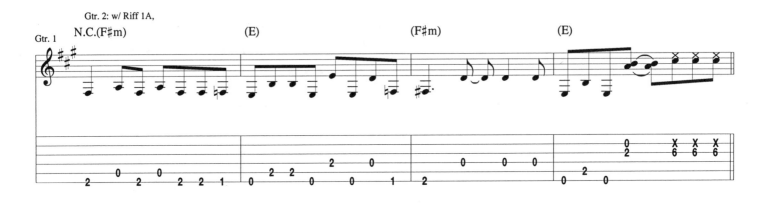

Guitar Solo

Gtr. 2: w/ Riff 1A, 4 times

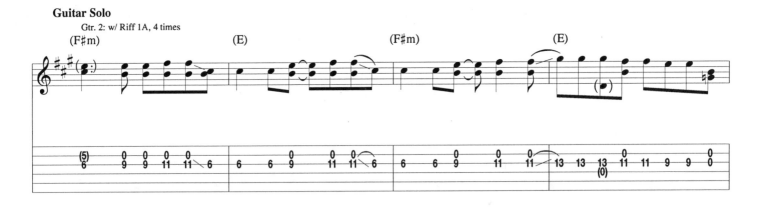

D.S. al Coda
(2nd ending)

Coda

No, I don't __ have a gun. __ No, I don't __

Gtr. 2: w/ Riff 1A, 2 times

Mem - o - ry, __

Gtr. 1

a... __   rit.

rit.

Jesus Doesn't Want Me For A Sunbeam

Words and Music by Frances McKee and Eugene Kelly

Chorus

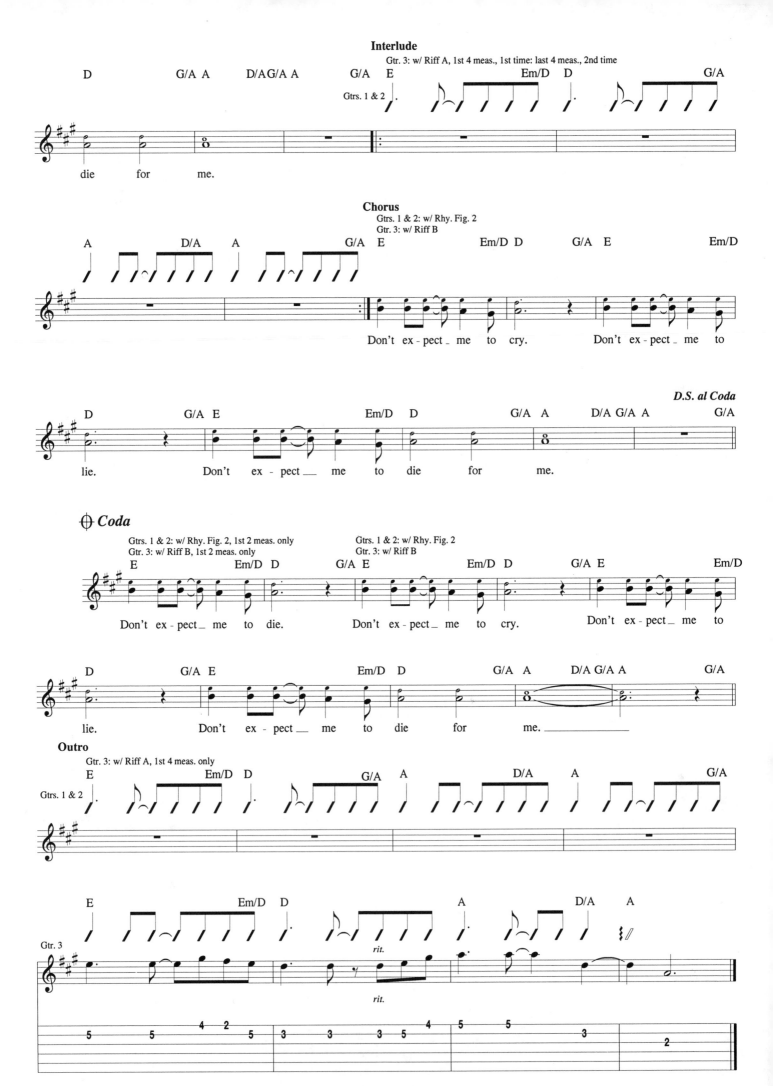

The Man Who Sold The World

Words and Music by David Bowie

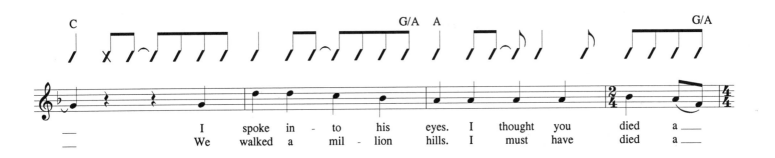

I spoke in-to his eyes. I thought you died a ___
We walked a mil-lion hills. I must have died a ___

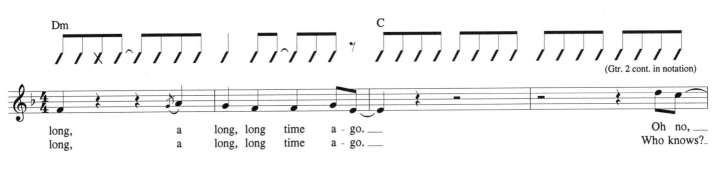

long, a long, long time a-go. ___
long, a long, long time a-go. ___

Oh no, ___
Who knows? ___

(Gtr. 2 cont. in notation)

%. Chorus

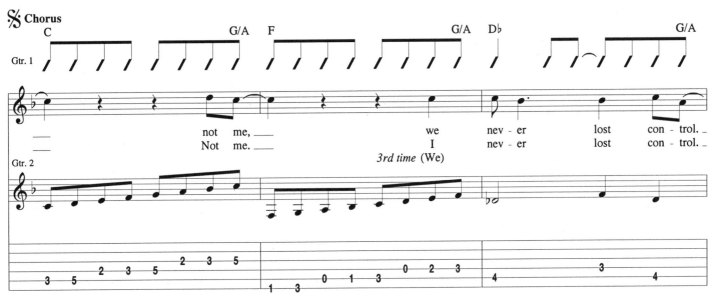

Gtr. 1

not me, ___ we nev-er lost con-trol. ___
Not me. ___ I nev-er lost con-trol. ___

Gtr. 2

3rd time (We)

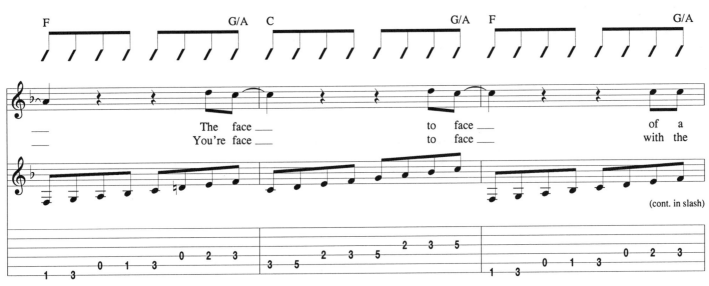

The face ___ to face ___ of a
You're face ___ to face ___ with the

(cont. in slash)

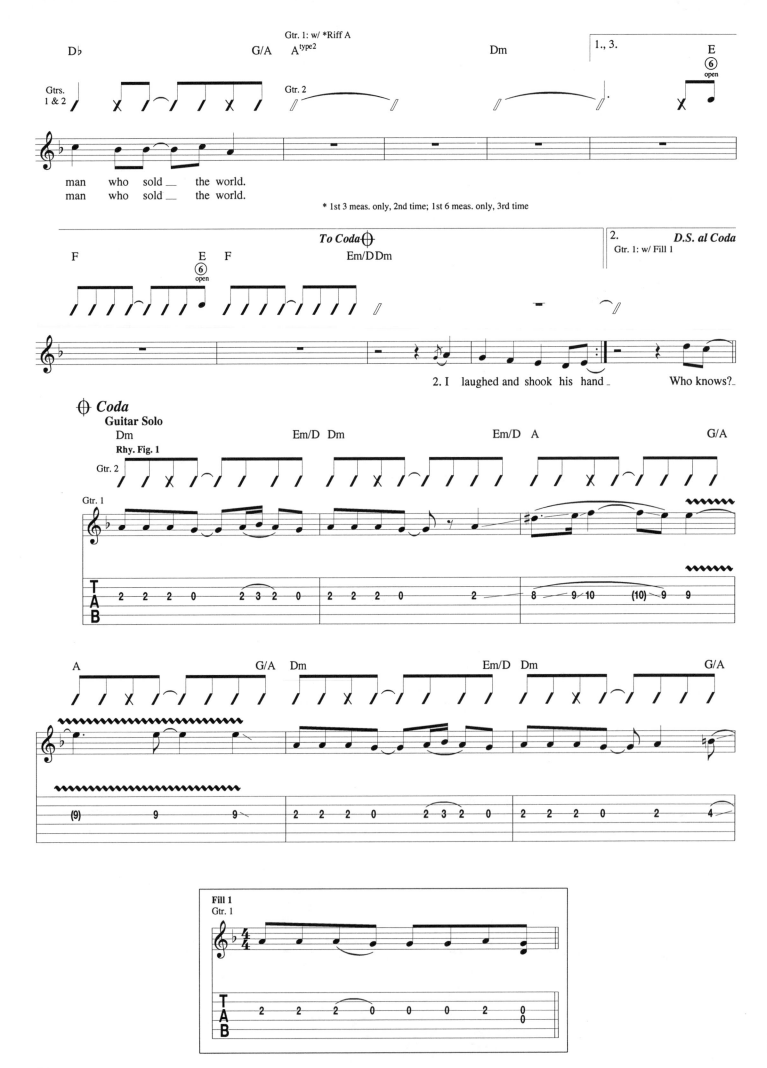

man who sold __ the world.
man who sold __ the world.

* 1st 3 meas. only, 2nd time; 1st 6 meas. only, 3rd time

2. I laughed and shook his hand __ Who knows? __

Coda
Guitar Solo

Fill 1
Gtr. 1

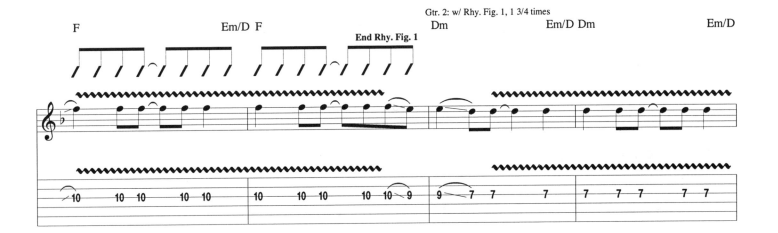

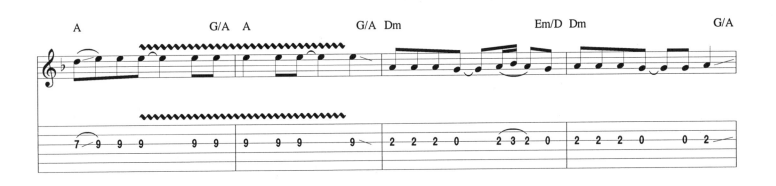

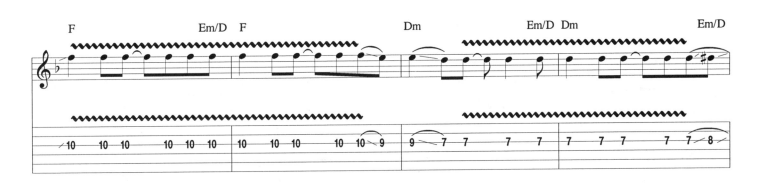

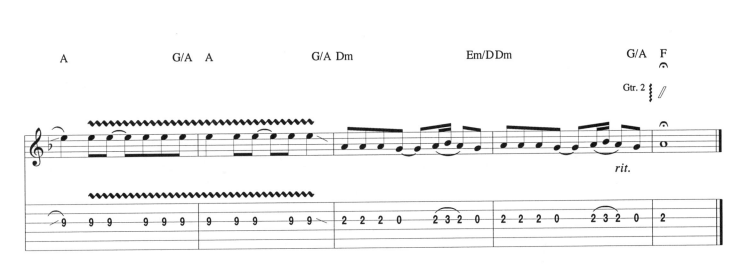

Penny Royal Tea

Words and Music by Kurt Cobain

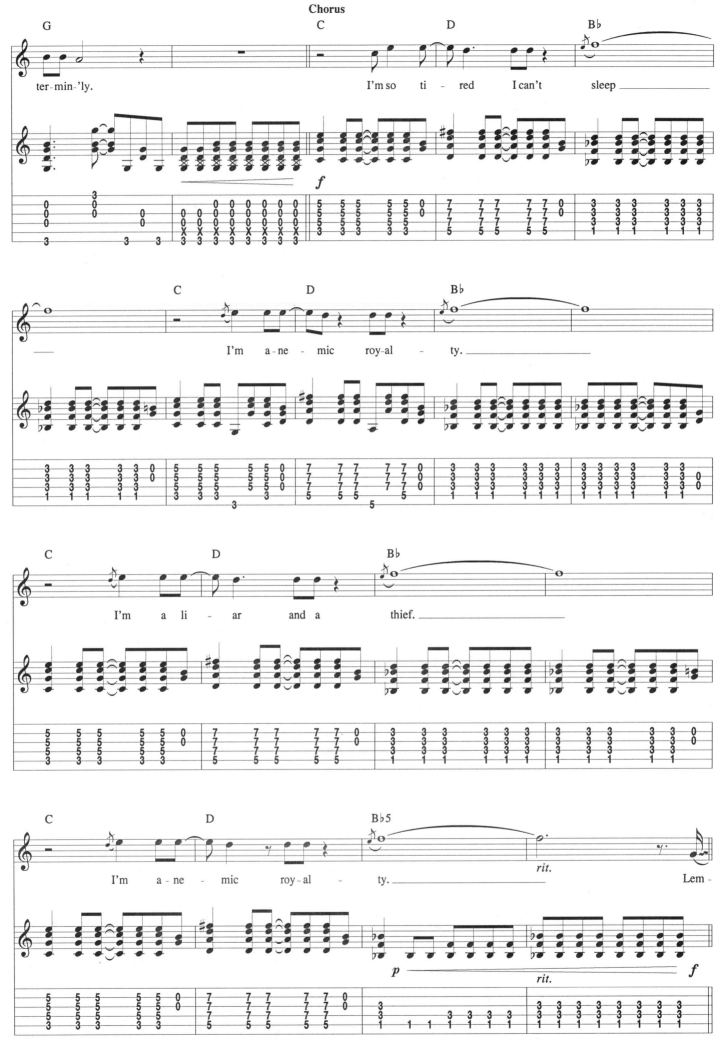

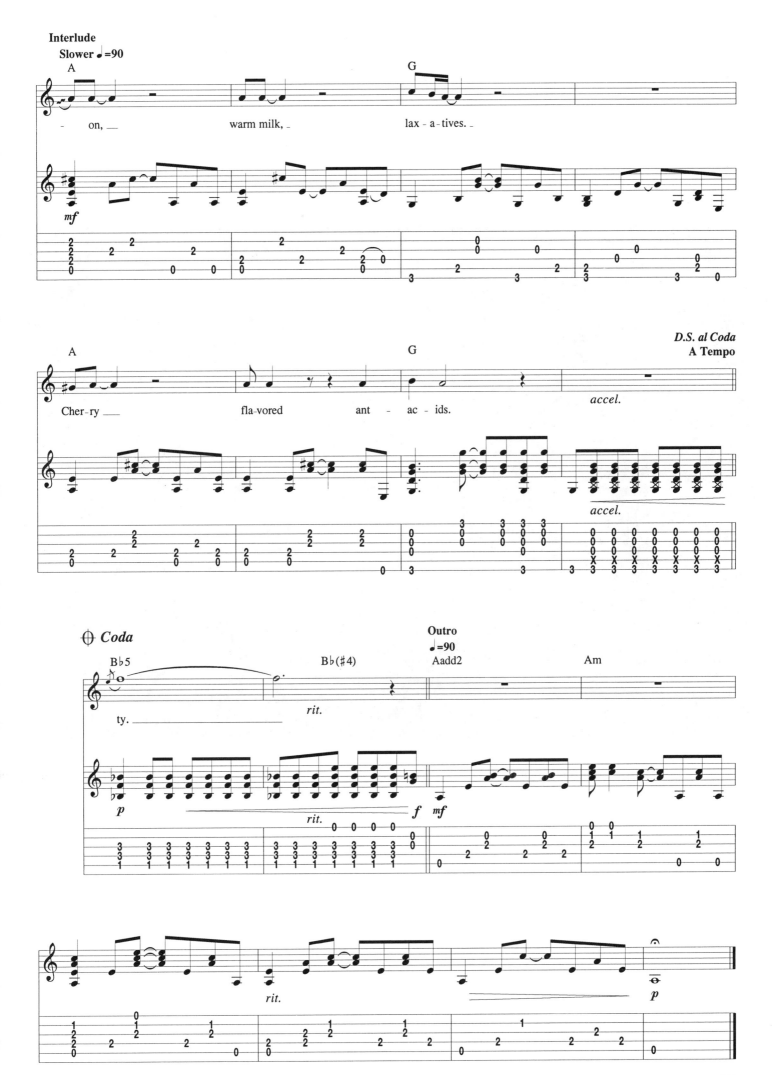

Dumb

Music and Words by Kurt Cobain

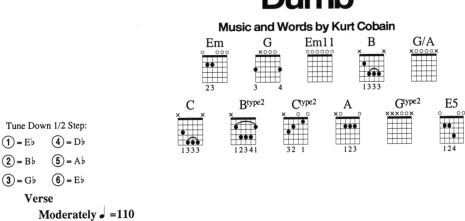

Tune Down 1/2 Step:

① = Eb   ④ = Db
② = Bb   ⑤ = Ab
③ = Gb   ⑥ = Eb

Verse

Moderately ♩ =110

Gtr. 3: w/ Fill 1, 2nd time

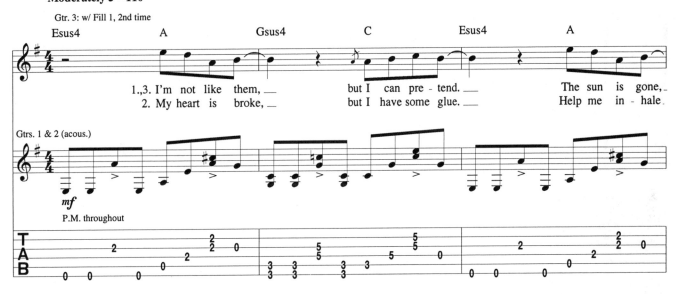

Esus4 / A / Gsus4 / C / Esus4 / A

1.,3. I'm not like them, __ but I can pre-tend. __ The sun is gone, __
2. My heart is broke, __ but I have some glue. __ Help me in-hale.

Gtrs. 1 & 2 (acous.)

mf

P.M. throughout

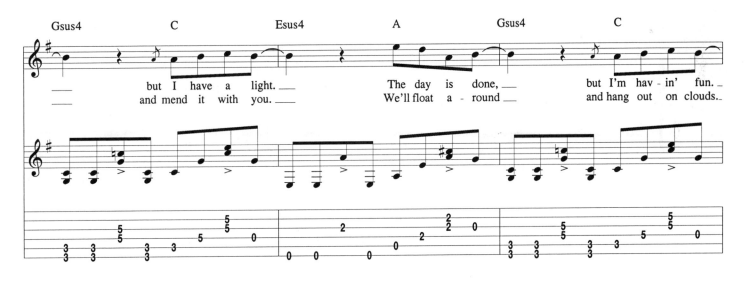

Gsus4 / C / Esus4 / A / Gsus4 / C

__ but I have a light. __ The day is done, __ but I'm hav-in' fun. __
__ and mend it with you. __ We'll float a-round __ and hang out on clouds. __

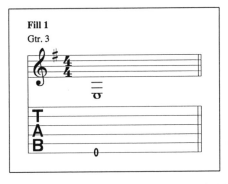

Fill 1

Gtr. 3

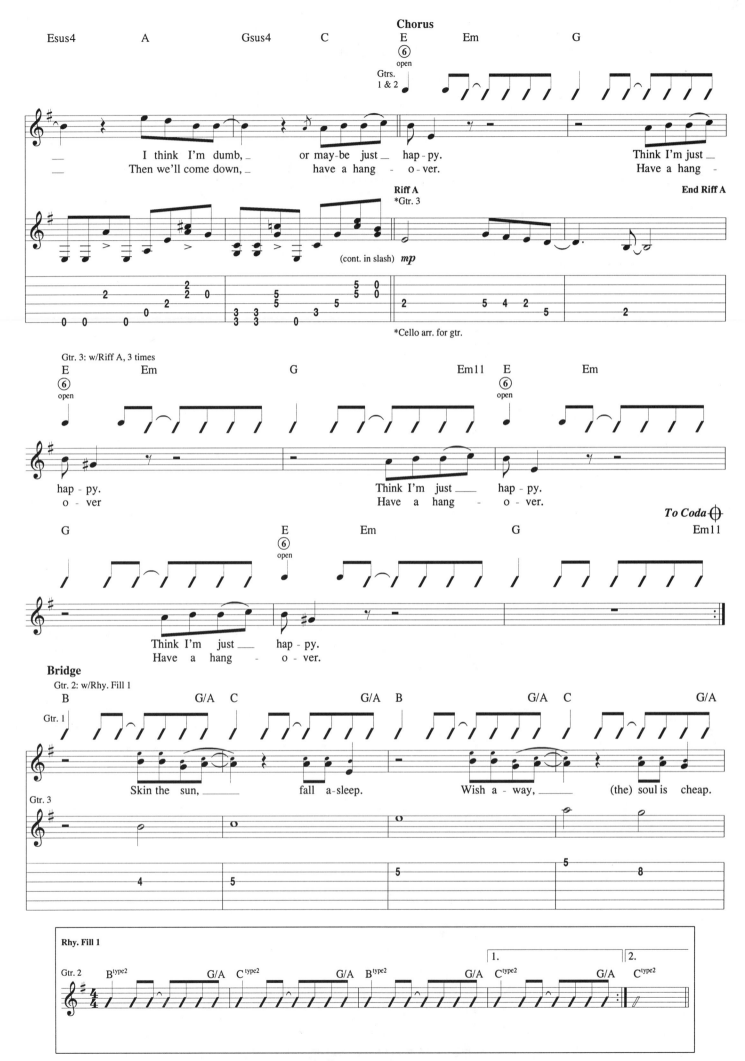

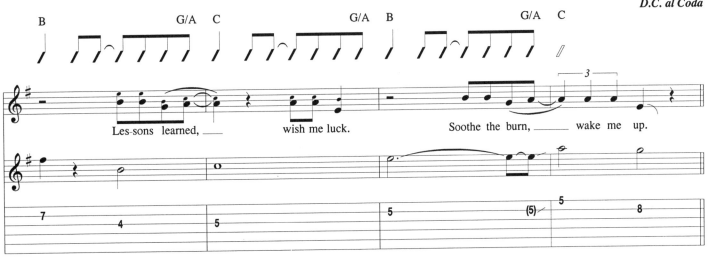

⊕ *Coda*

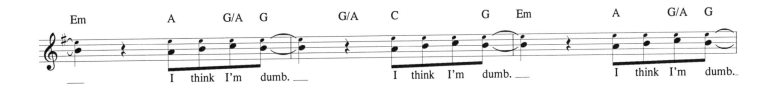

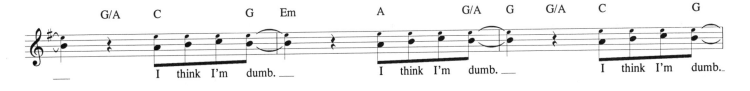

(New Wave) Polly

By Kurt Cobain

your dirt - y wings. _ Let me take a ride. _ Don't hurt your - self. _ I want some help _

to help my - self. _ I've got some rope, _ you have been told. _ I prom-ise you _

I have been true. _ Let me take a ride. _ Don't hurt your - self. _ I want some help _

To Coda ⊕ | 1.

Gtrs. 1 & 2: w/ Rhy. Fig. 1, 2 times

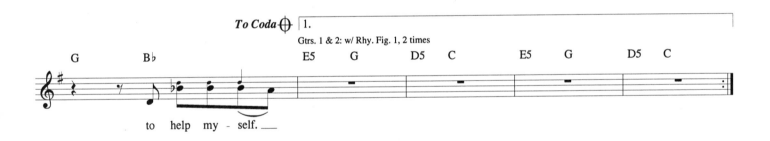

to help my - self. _

| 2.

D.S. al Coda

⊕ *Coda*

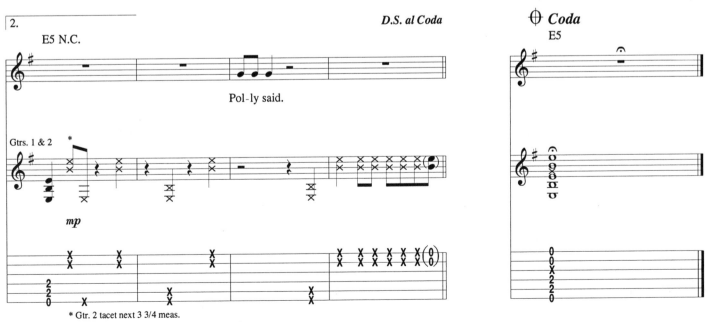

Pol-ly said.

Gtrs. 1 & 2

mp

* Gtr. 2 tacet next 3 3/4 meas.

On A Plain

Words and Music by Kurt Cobain

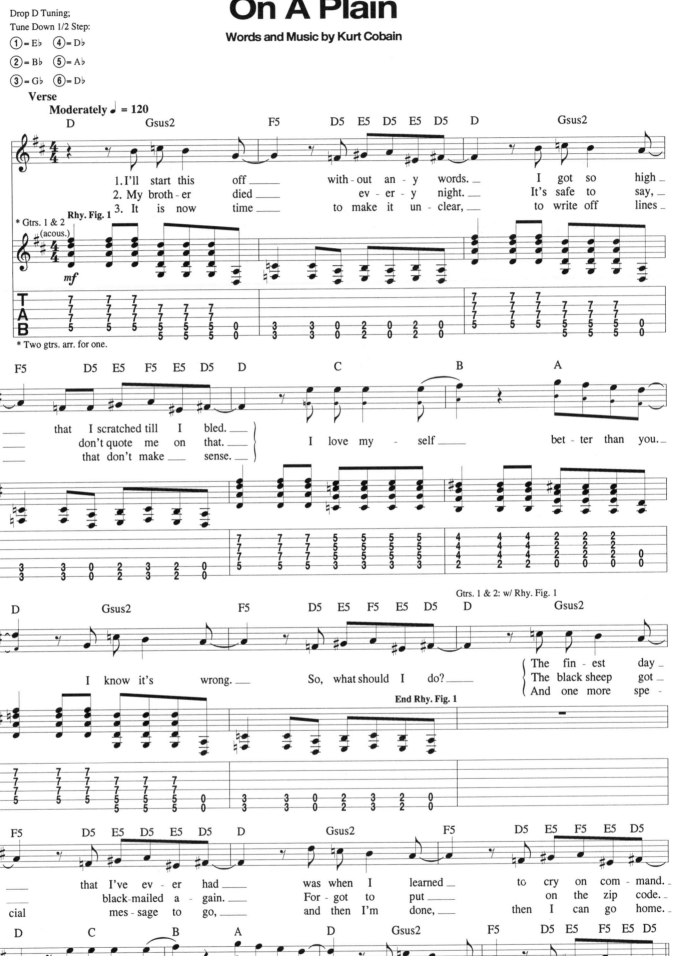

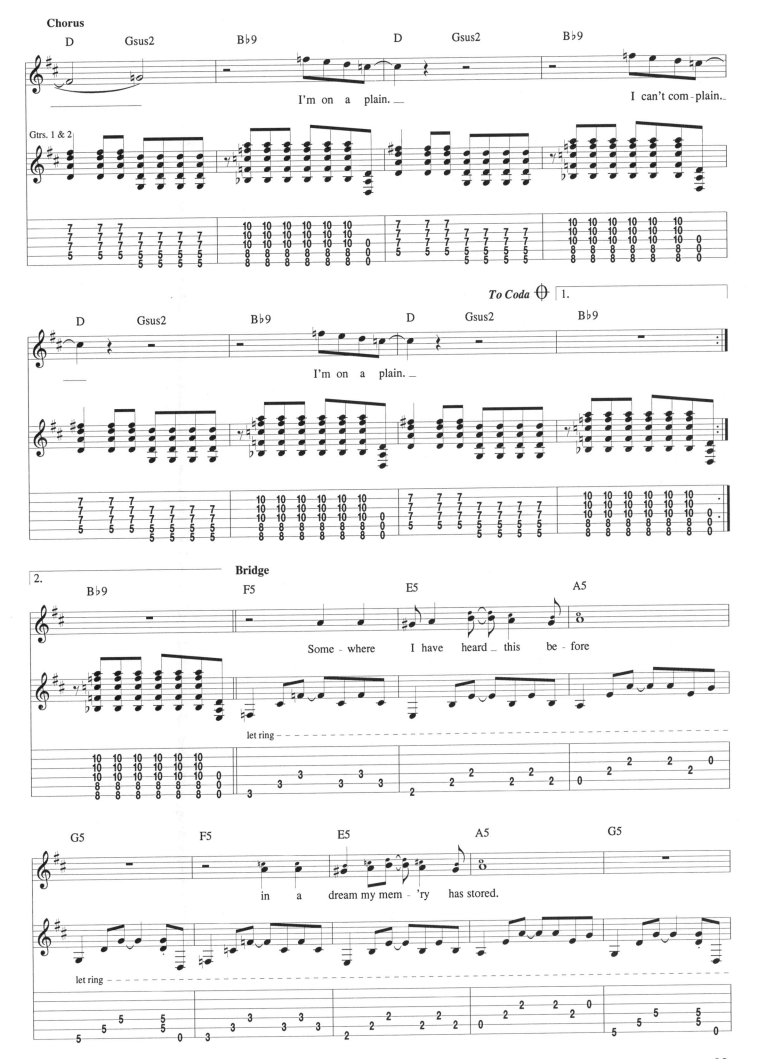

Something In The Way

By Kurt Cobain

Drop D Tuning;
Tune Down 1/2 Step:

① = Eb ④ = Db
② = Bb ⑤ = Ab
③ = Gb ⑥ = Db

Intro

Slow and Mysterious ♩ = 54

Gtr. 1 (acous.) F#5   D5   F#5   D5

mf

let ring throughout

Verse

F#5   D5   N.C. (F#m)   D5

1. Un-der - neath _ the bridge, _ the tarp has sprung _ a leak. _ And the

F#5   D5   F#5   D5

an - i - mals _ I've trapped _ have all be - come _ my pets. _ And I'm

it's o - kay ___ to eat fish, ___ 'cause they don't have an - y feel - ings. ___

⊕ *Coda*

Mm. _____ Some-thing in the way. ___ Mm. _____

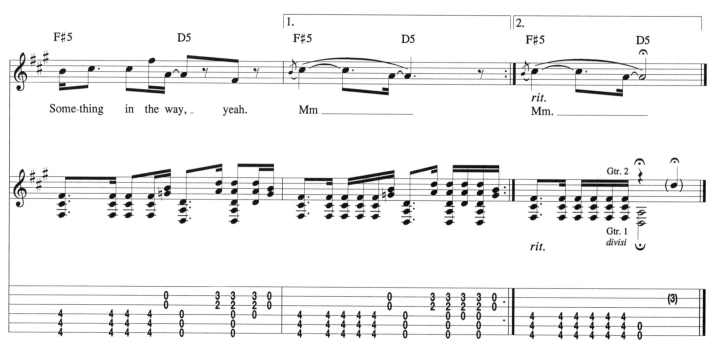

Some-thing in the way, ___ yeah. Mm _____ Mm. _____

1.

2.

rit.

Gtr. 2

Gtr. 1
divisi

rit.

Plateau

Words and Music by Curt Kirkwood

Verse

Gtr. 1: w/ Rhy. Fig. 1, 4 times

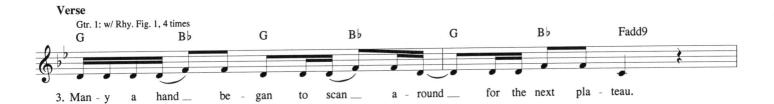

3. Man - y a hand __ be - gan to scan __ a - round __ for the next pla - teau.

Some say __ it was Green-land and some say Mex - i - co. __ Oth-ers de-cid - ed it __ was no - where, ex -

cept for where they stood. Those were all __ just guess - es, __ would-n't help you if they could.

Outro

Ooh, ooh. __ Ooh, ooh. __

simile on repeats

let ring throughout

Oh Me

Words and Music by Curt Kirkwood

Guitar Solo

D.S. al Coda

2. If I had to lose a

Coda

-side me. _____ Form-u-late af - fin - i - ty _____ in -

P.M.

Lake Of Fire

Words and Music by Curt Kirkwood

All Apologies

Words and Music by Kurt Cobain

Drop D Tuning;
Tune Down 1/2 Step:
①= E♭ ④= D♭
②= B♭ ⑤= A♭
③= G♭ ⑥= D♭

Intro
Moderately ♩ = 109

Verse

Gtr. 2: w/ Rhy. Fig. 1A, 4 times, simile

N.C.(D)

1. What else should I be? ___ All a-pol - o-gies. ___
2. I wish I was like you, ___ eas - i - ly ___ a - mused. ___

What else should I say? __ Ev - 'ry-one __ is gay. __
Find my nest of salt. __ Ev - 'ry-thing __ is my fault. __

What else should I write? __ I don't have __ the right. __
I'll take all the blame, __ aq - ua sea - foam shame. __

What else should I be? __ All a - pol - o - gies. __
Sun-burn, (with) freez - er - burn. __ Chok - ing on __ the ash - es of her en - e - my.

(cont. in slash)

Chorus

G

Gtrs. 1 & 2

simile on repeat

In the sun, __ in the sun __ I feel __ as one. __

In the sun _____ in the sun... _____ (I'm)

Gtr. 1: w/ Fill 1, 2nd time

A

Gtr. 2

mar - ried, _____ bur - ied. _____

Gtr. 1

Fill 1
Gtr. 1

N.C.(D)

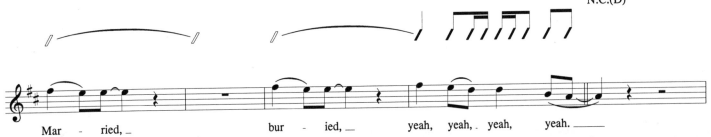

Mar - ried, ___ bur - ied, ___ yeah, yeah, yeah, yeah. _____

* Gtrs. 1 & 2: w/ Rhy. Figs. 1 & 1A, simile

play 4 times

All a - lone ___ is all ___ we all ___ are. All a - lone ___ is all ___ we all ___ are.

* Gtr. 2 fades out 4th time.

Gtr. 2 tacet
N.C.(D)

All a - lone ___ is all ___ we all. ___ are. All a - lone ___ is all ___ we all ___ are.

Gtr. 1

All a - lone ___ is all ___ we all... ___ All a - lone ___ is all ___ we all ___ are.

Gtr. 1 tacet

All a - lone _____ is all _____ we all _____ are.

Where Did You Sleep Last Night

New Words and New Music Adaptation by Huddie Ledbetter

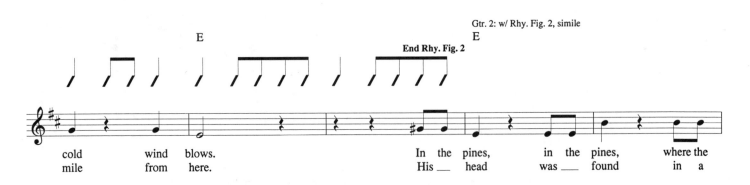

sun   don't ev - er shine,   I would shiv - er ____ the whole   night through.   3. The
driv - ing wheel,   but his bod - y ____ nev - er was found.   4. My

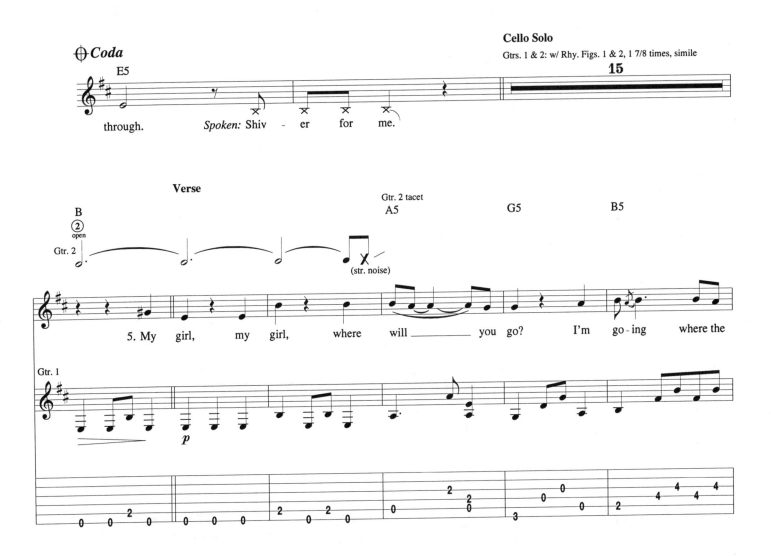

⊕ *Coda*

Cello Solo
Gtrs. 1 & 2: w/ Rhy. Figs. 1 & 2, 1 7/8 times, simile

15

through.   *Spoken:* Shiv - er   for   me.

Verse

Gtr. 2 tacet

5. My   girl,   my   girl,   where   will ____ you go?   I'm   go - ing   where the

Gtr. 1

cold   wind blows.   In the pines,   in the pines,   where the sun   don't ev - er

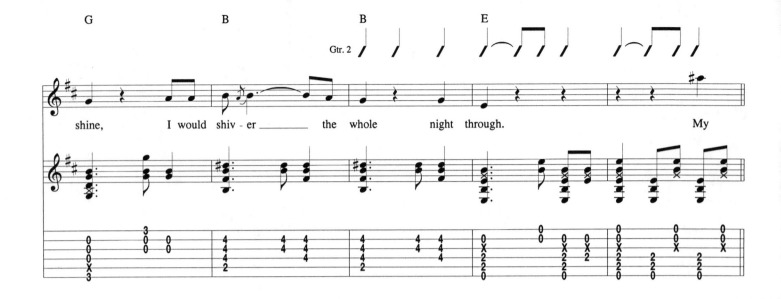

shine, I would shiv - er _____ the whole night through. My

Outro
Gtrs. 1 & 2: w/ Rhy. Figs. 1 & 2, 3 1/2 times, simile

girl, my girl, don't lie _____ to me. Tell me, where did you sleep last

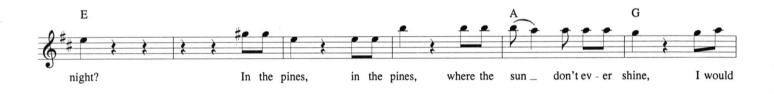

night? In the pines, in the pines, where the sun _ don't ev - er shine, I would

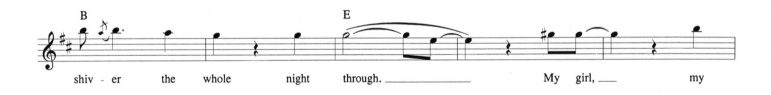

shiv - er the whole night through. _____ My girl, ___ my

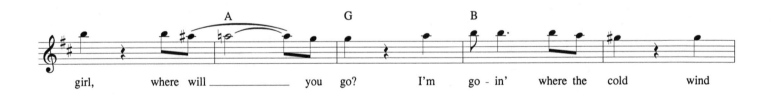

girl, where will _____ you go? I'm go - in' where the cold wind

blows. In the pines, the pines, the sun don't shine, I'd

Free-Time

Gtrs. 1 & 2 tacet

A Tempo

shiv - er _____ the whole ___ night through. _____

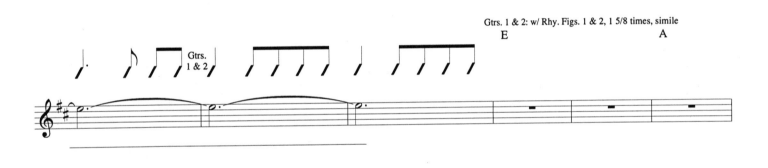

Gtrs. 1 & 2: w/ Rhy. Figs. 1 & 2, 1 5/8 times, simile

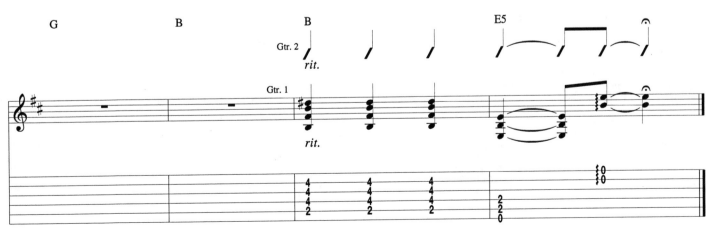

NOTATION LEGEND